W9-CCR-487

YOU CAN BE A WOMAN MARINE BIOLOGIST

Florence McAlary
and
Judith Love Cohen

Illustrations:
David A. Katz

Editing:
Janice J. Martin

Cascade
Pass, Inc.

www.cascadepass.com

Copyright © 1992 and 2001 by Cascade Pass, Inc.
Published by Cascade Pass, Inc., Suite C-105, 4223 Glencoe Avenue
Marina del Rey, CA 90292-8801
Phone (310) 305-0210
Printed in Hong Kong by South China Printing Co. (1988) Ltd.

Revised Edition 2001
You Can Be a Woman Marine Biologist was written by Florence McAlary and Judith
Love Cohen, designed and illustrated by David Katz, and edited by Janice Martin.

This book is one of a series that emphasizes the value of science and mathematical
studies by depicting real women whose careers provide inspirational role models.

Other books in the series include:
You Can Be A Woman Engineer   *You Can Be A Woman Oceanographer*
You Can Be A Woman Architect   *You Can Be A Woman Astronomer*
You Can Be A Woman Paleontologist   *You Can Be A Woman Cardiologist*
You Can Be A Woman Zoologist   *You Can Be A Woman Botanist*
You Can Be A Woman Egyptologist

Library of Congress Cataloging-in-Publication Data
McAlary, Florence Aleen.
      You can be a woman marine biologist / Florence McAlary and Judith Love
Cohen ; illustrations, David A. Katz ; edited by Janice J. Martin. -- Rev. ed.
         p.   cm.
      Summary: Describes what a career in marine biology is like, using examples
from the life of research scientist Dr. Florence McAlary.
      ISBN 1-880599-54-6 (hardcover) -- ISBM 1-880599-53-8 (pbk.)
      1. Marine Biology--Vocational guidance--Juvenile literature. 2. Vocational
guidance for women--Juvenile literature. 3. McAlary, Florence Aleen--Juvenile
literature. [1. Marine biology--Vocational guidance. 2. McAlary, Florence Aleen. 3.
Marine biologists. 4. Women--Biography. 5. Vocational guidance. 6. Occupations.]
I. Cohen, Judith Love, 1933-   . II. Katz, David A. (David Arthur), 1949-   ill.
III. Martin, Janice J. IV. Title.
         QH91.16 .M43   2001   2001047046
         578.77'023--dc21

Dedication

This book is dedicated to Elsa Katz, who taught her children and friends to love the ocean and to respect all forms of life, and to Jeanne McAlary McFarland and all of the young women whose choices will make a difference in the future of our oceans.

The diver is drifting very quietly with the current in the clear water, checking the compass and making slight corrections to the course. Sea mounts appear ahead. Suddenly, the diver sees dark shadows approaching. When Florence McAlary looks up, she sees a hammerhead shark, and then another and another. Her heart beats a little faster. But the whole school swims past her peacefully, just the way she likes it.

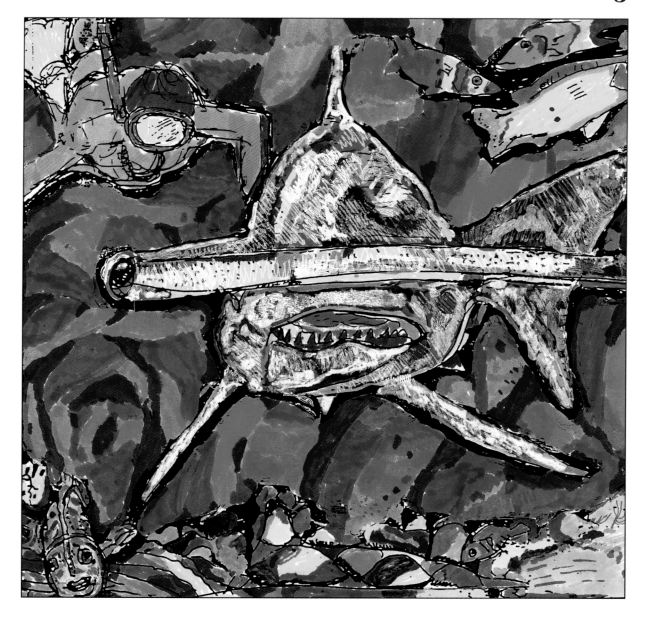

The Dr. McAlary is in the Sea of Cortez in Baja, California. She is here with other scientists to photograph and inventory marine life. Whether searching for sharks, gazing at "gardens" of snake-like eel fish, exploring for corals by moonlight, or beach-walking to investigate a fisherman's catch . . . she will come to know this unique place. Florence will do her best to use her knowledge to protect this special wilderness: the ocean. This is Dr. Florence McAlary's story.

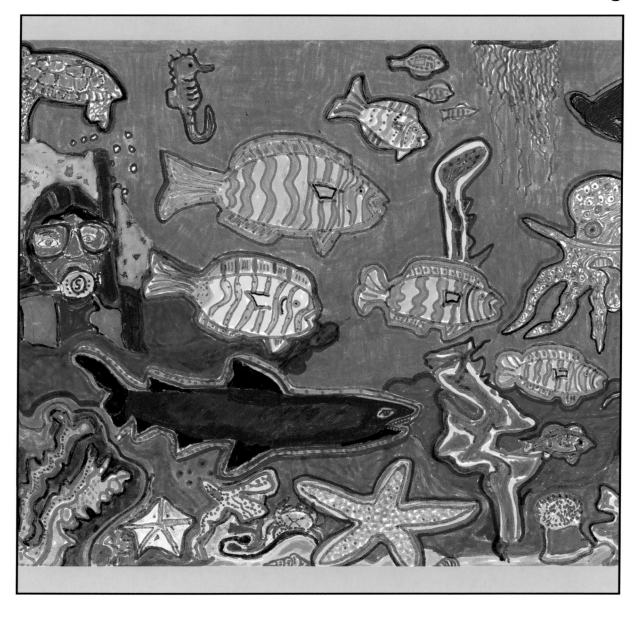

When I was a little girl, I loved to go fishing on the beach with my grandfather. He would fish; I would collects shells, find little crabs running in and out of the sand, and look at tide pools. I was always curious about living things.

I have fond memories of camping with my family in national parks like Yosemite. I loved the wilderness. The forest rangers would lead us on walks and talk about the animals and plants. I wanted very much to be a ranger naturalist, but I was frightened by the bears at night . . . .

I loved working with living things. Maybe I could be a doctor or a nurse? But I really loved animals.

I studied general biology in college and was still undecided. And then I took a course called "herpetology"; it was about lizards and snakes and frogs. I camped in the desert with other students in order to observe these animals in their natural environment.

Later I traveled to other wild places: the Serengeti Plain in Africa and the Amazon jungle.

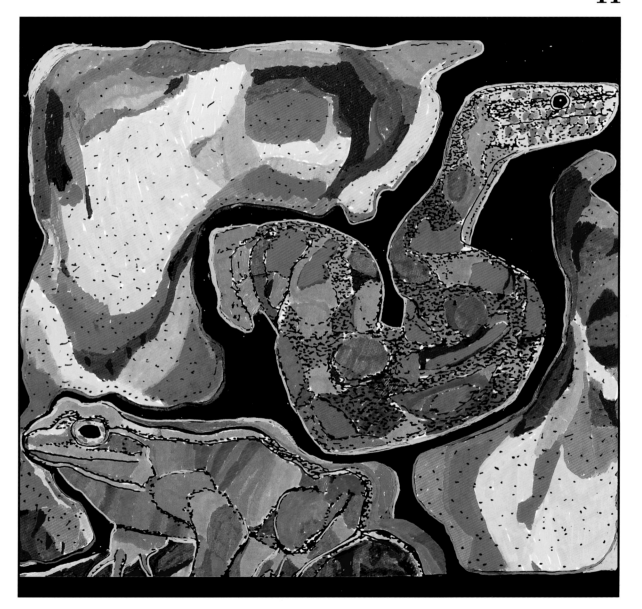

I loved the wilderness and wanted to help preserve it. I found my subject, but the habitat I finally chose to study was quite different.

My wilderness was to be under water: the kelp beds and the coral reefs. I would learn to scuba dive. I was going to be a marine biologist!

First, I studied about all the living things.

Biology begins by classifying and naming things in Latin. There are two major kingdoms: the plant kingdom and the animal kingdom (fungi and bacteria and other single-celled life forms now have their own kingdoms).

The plant kingdom (kingdom Plantae) contains groups such as large algae (seaweed) and seed-bearing plants such as trees and flowering plants.

The animal kingdom (kingdom Animalia) contains groups such as Mollusca (shellfish) and Chordata (vertebrates such as fish, amphibians and mammals).

A main group is called a phylum, a subgroup is called a class. In each class there can be an order, a family, a genus and a species. The Latin names help to describe the plants and animals being classified.

Second, I studied about living things in their environments.

Ecology is the study of the relationship between animals and plants and their surroundings. A group of animals and plants that live together is known as a community. The place where they live is called their habitat. A tropical forest or a kelp forest are examples of habitats.

Finally, I got to concentrate on marine biology, the study of living things in the sea.

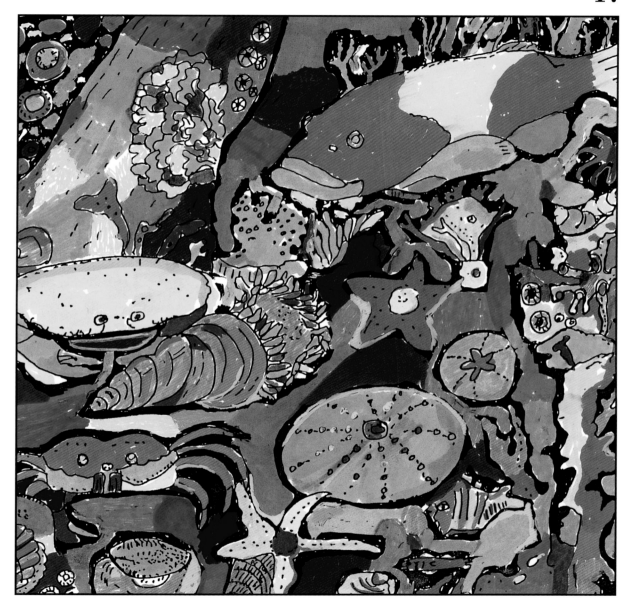

Now that I knew what marine biology was, I had to learn how to do.

I learned about the scientific method and how it is used by biologists.

First, you observe nature and notice things that you are curious about. You ask questions; then you try to devise possible answers to your questions. This usually involves a "hunch" called a hypothesis. Then you conduct experiments or tests to try out your hunch. Finally, you come up with your answers.

When I was studying damselfish in the Virgin Islands, I noticed that fish eggs that were there in the afternoon were gone by the next morning. How did the fish eggs hatch during the night?

My hunch (hypothesis) was that darkness triggered the hatching of the baby fish.

I designed two different tests. They both involved collecting eggs from the nests of tropical coral reef damselfish. The damselfish's common name is Sergeant Major. Its full list of Latin names (its classification) which describes its characteristics is: kingdom *Animalia*, phylum *Chordata*, subphylum *Vertebrata*, class *Osteichthyes*, order *Perciformes*, family *Pomacentridae*, genus *Abudefduf*, species *saxatalis*. Biologists don't take short cuts!

For the first test, my colleagues and I put the eggs in light-proof cans. For the second test, we shined lights on the eggs.

At the end of ten minutes, we opened one can and counted the number of hatched eggs. We continued to open cans every ten minutes and count the eggs.

And then we studied the results. The eggs in the dark cans all hatched in 60 minutes. And the ones that had light on them didn't hatch at all.

Our conclusion: Darkness is essential to the hatching of damselfish eggs.

Remember, the scientific method has three steps:

1. Your observation and your questions which lead to your hunch or hypothesis.
2. Your test or experiment.
3. Your result or conclusion.

How can you tell if you would be good at marine biology? If you can answer yes to the following questions, then you should consider becoming a marine.

    1. Do you like asking and answering questions?
       Are you curious? Do you like being curious?

I wanted to know how and why seastars grew a whole new star from a single ray (a ray is one of the seastar's five arms); how many sea urchins lived in the kelp forest, and did they affect how well the kelp grew? I loved asking questions and finding answers to them.

2. Do you like animals and all living things?
Do you collect caterpillars, grow plants, like to
watch fish, birds, and lizards?

I love the fish and plants I see every day where I now work, in the waters of the Pacific Northwest. I want these fish and plants (even the sharks) to be here and healthy for my children and my grandchildren to enjoy.

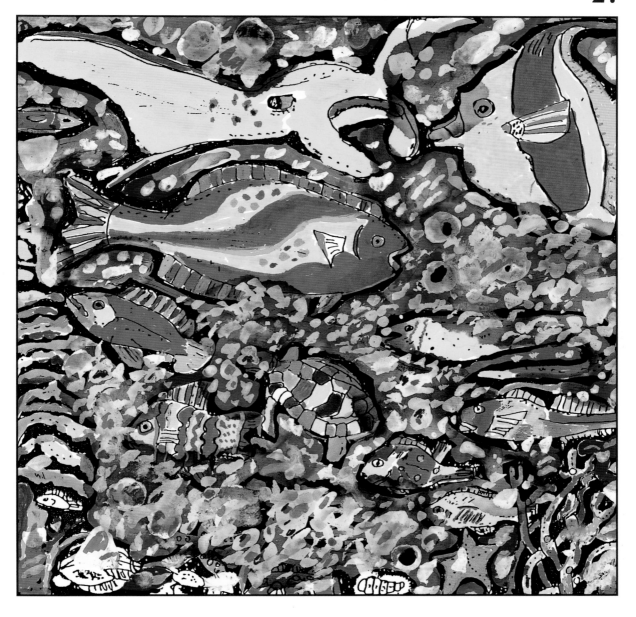

3. Are you adventurous? Do you want to go out into the wilderness? Do you enjoy being out in nature and seeing it all first-hand?

I thoroughly enjoy being under the water in the kelp or the coral. But you don't have to scuba or even swim to be a marine biologist. Many of us stay on the boat and study samples under a microscope. But you do need to venture out to where the marine wildlife is: Santa Catalina Island, Virgin Islands, Hawaii, Galapagos Islands, Key West . . . wherever the sea offers a particularly interesting habitat.

The high points of my career have been my contributions to saving the wilderness. My work with the Channel Islands National Park included drilling holes in rock to secure weighted lines through the kelp forest. We marine biologists use these "grids," together with photographs, to make counts of individual species and to find out how many kelp plants, abalone, lobsters, seastars, sea urchins and fish are there. We compare our results from the current year with counts done the previous year.

In this way we will know if the kelp forest populations of plants or animals are decreasing, remaining the same, or increasing.

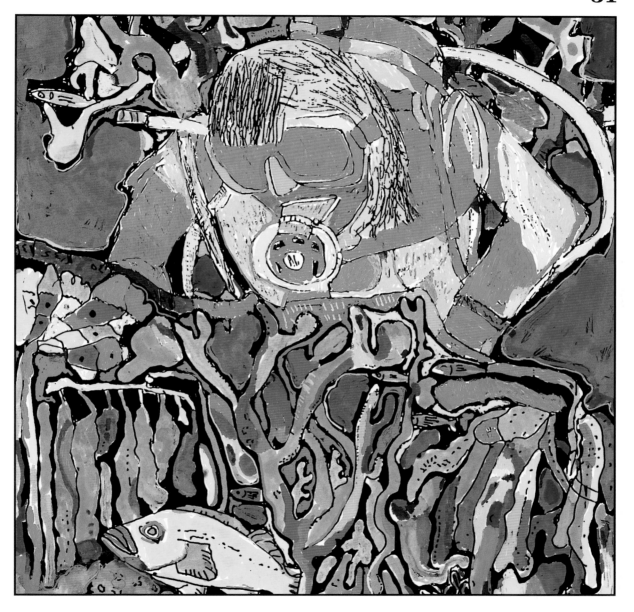

I also particularly enjoy reconnaissance cruises where we try to name everything we find: algae, fish, invertebrates. We make an inventory for future generations to see how the environments change with time and whether pollution or over-fishing are a problem. Sometimes, we even discover a new species.

If you like living things, if you are curious and want to know things, and if you want to keep the beauty and variety of the wilderness for future generations, then you can do it too. You can be a woman marine biologist!

SCIENCE LESSON PLAN 1

PURPOSE: To understand how species in an ocean habitat have specific roles and special adaptations for survival.

MATERIALS: Mural-sized paper, art supplies (crayons, paint, colored pencils, glitter, etc.), scissors, glue.

PROCEDURES: Have children plan and construct a mural to illustrate plants and animals in a specific marine ecosystem (e.g., rocky intertidal, coral reef, kelp forest, wetlands, Antarctic).

CONCLUSIONS: Where in the world is your ecosystem?
What kinds of fish and plants live in this habitat?
How do the colors and shapes of fish relate to their habitat?
Which are the predators and what do they eat?
Compare the shapes and colors with those that live in other ecosystems.

RESOURCES: Posters, textbooks on marine biology or specific ocean communities, magazine articles. Visit a local marine aquarium. Take a trip to a habitat (e.g., wetlands).

SCIENCE LESSON PLAN 2

PURPOSE: Develop an understanding of the classification of marine plants and animals.

MATERIALS: Bendable wire, string, pictures of marine plants and animals (magazines, calandars), scissors, glue, art supplies, construction paper.

PROCEDURES: Have the children construct mobiles using pasted pictures, drawings, or cutouts of marine plants and animals to illustrate different themes in marine classification.

Choose a theme such as: families of fish, orders of marine mammals, members of a class such as Chondricthyes (sharks and rays), members of phyla such as the ones that contain sponges, corals, jellyfish, seastars, marine birds, etc.

CONCLUSIONS: What theme did you select and why?
How does your mobile illustrate the theme you chose?
What kind of animals belong to the classification you chose? How are the animals different from each other?

SCIENCE LESSON PLAN 3

PURPOSE: To develop a dynamic understanding of marine food webs.

MATERIALS: Spacious environment.

PROCEDURES: Have the children describe a marine food chain and select a different sound for each plant and animal. As a group practice the sounds and the names of the plants or animals. Assign the children their own specific plant or animal (more than one child can have the same plant or animal).

Have the children spread out, close their eyes and make their sounds while listening for the sounds of others. Very slowly the children should start to take little steps and search for their own kind and the kind of food they eat. When they find either one they should hold hands and keep looking. After a period of time the teacher calls out "Stop searching," and the children open their eyes and see the results.

CONCLUSIONS: Was it hard to find your own kind? What functions do the sounds have?
Were you captured by your predator? How could you avoid being captured?

RESOURCES: Recordings of sounds in the sea.

About the Authors:

Dr. Florence McAlary is now Dr. Florence McAlary is a research scientist affiliated with the Friday Harbor marine Laboratory (University of Washington) on San Juan Island, Washington. She received her doctorate in biology and her master's and bachelor's degrees in zoology from the University of California at Los Angeles. Among her favorite times are the five years she spent at the Wrigley Institute for Environmental Science (University of Southern California) on Catalina Island teaching and studying seastars and fish. Her publications include contributions to the California Islands Symposia on kelp forest monitoring, twilight behavior of marine fish and invertebrates, and the population biology of a fissiparous seastar. Additionally, she is a certified diver and skilled underwater photographer. Dr. McAlary and her husband currently study the feeding behavior of juvenile fish. She is active in professional organizations and with her daughter in 4H and Pony Club. Her hobbies include skiing, horseback riding, bird-watching and reading.

Judith Love Cohen is a Registered Professional Electrical Engineer with bachelor's and master's degrees in engineering from the University of Southern California and University of California at Los Angeles. She has written plays, screenplays, and newspaper articles in addition to her series of children's books that began with *You Can Be a Woman Engineer*.

About the Illustrator:

David Arthur Katz received his training in art education and holds a master's degree from the University of South Florida. He is a credentialed teacher in the Los Angeles Unified School District. His involvement in the arts has included animation, illustration, and play-, poetry- and song-writing.